Patience and Humility

William Bernard
Ullathorne, O.S.B.

Patience and Humility

A Handbook for Christians

SOPHIA INSTITUTE PRESS®
Manchester, New Hampshire

Patience and Humility: A Handbook for Christians contains selections from William Bernard Ullathorne's *The Groundwork of the Christian Virtues* and *Christian Patience*. It was originally published in London in 1908 by Burns and Oates under the title *The Little Book of Humility and Patience* and later published by The Newman Bookshop in Westminster, Maryland, in 1945. This 1998 edition by Sophia Institute Press includes slight editorial revisions throughout the text.

Copyright © 1998 Sophia Institute Press®

Printed in the United States of America

All rights reserved

Jacket design by Lorraine Bilodeau

The cover painting is a detail of *The Young Draftsman Carle Vernet* by Nicholas Bernard Lepicie, in the Louvre, Paris, France. (Scala / Art Resource, New York).

Sophia Institute Press®

Box 5284, Manchester, NH 03108

1-800-888-9344

Library of Congress Cataloging-in-Publication Data

Ullathorne, William Bernard, 1806-1889.
    [Little book of humility and patience]
    Patience and humility : a handbook for Christians / William
    Bernard Ullathorne.
        p. cm.
    Originally published: The little book of humility and patience.
    London : Burns and Oates, 1908.
    ISBN 0-918477-74-3 (pbk. : alk. paper)
    1. Humility — Christianity. 2. Patience — Religious aspects —
    Christianity. I. Title.
BV4647.H8U44 1998
241'.4 — dc21   98-19804 CIP

01 02 10 9 8 7 6 5 4 3

Contents

Virtue

Humility

Patience

Patience and Humility

Editor's Note: The biblical references in the following pages are based on the Douay-Rheims version of the Old and New Testaments. Where applicable, quotations have been cross-referenced with the differing names and enumeration in the Revised Standard Version, using the following symbol: (RSV =).

Virtue

Surrender your will to God

Spiritual natures are on the summits of creation; there is nothing but God above them.

There is no master so large-minded, so generous, or so well acquainted with you and your requirements as God; no father so loving and bountiful; no friend so free from all jealousy; none who so completely loves you for your greater good. While there is no tyrant so narrow-minded, so proudhearted, so exacting, so suspicious, so utterly bent on keeping you to your own littleness, as the one we all know so well, of whose tyranny we have had such bitter experience, and who goes by the name of Myself. Yet God or yourself you must choose for your master.

The whole design of God's beneficent government of souls is to draw them out of themselves and to bring them to His truth and good.

Patience and Humility

∞

This ever-moving earth is not only attracted to its own center, as all that constitutes man is held together by the central force of the soul, but it is held on its rapid course by the attraction of the sun; and as it turns toward that mighty luminary, it receives its image, and partakes of its light, warmth, and fertilizing power. Yet its rays are intercepted by the vapors which the earth produces, and by the turbulence arising from their conflicts.

And so by His creative influence does God hold the ever-active soul, in which He has placed His image, in its dependence. But when it turns its face with desire to Him who attracts it, He sends forth the celestial influence of His light, grace, and charity upon it, attracting it to move toward Him by faith, hope, and love, and it becomes a partaker of His goodness. But the soul is not necessitated like the earth, but free to make its choice. If it prefers its own central attraction, and the drawing to itself of the small things around it instead of the divine attraction, and its own uneasy love instead of divine love, then that soul is left to its own littleness, clouded and darkened by its own vapors, and troubled in itself.

Surrender your will to God

∽

Who can express the magnificence of the light of faith as compared with the light of reason? In the things of God and the soul, reason but gropes among the shadows reflected here below; while faith, with its direct light from God, opens out the infinite and eternal prospect of divine truth, which, although obscurely seen, is yet surely seen by the humble mind, giving a breadth and firmness to the mind that nothing can explain but the action of God in the soul.

God and His angels are near to the man of faith — so near that the gross veil of the body alone intervenes between our soul and the presence of God and our guardian angels.

∽

It is the fostering of minor troubles until they swell to a flood of sadness and discouragement that gives the Devil a turbid pool in which to cast his nets. If those minor troubles befall you, let them drop. Be not disturbed; turn your heart to God. Do not look at them; do not dispute with them; answer them not a word. Only turn your mind from them and let them drop.

∞

Only the power of God can bear us up to God. Our will is free, and if we follow the divine attraction, the grace of that attraction will bring us to His presence. But if we choose the attraction of these base and low things among which we are placed for our probation, and prefer the sordid limits of our nature to the heights of the divine goodness, we remain in the bonds of our disordered existence, distressed in spirit and far from God. The whole plan of our happiness is defeated from our want of generosity.

What does God ask of us? Not that we should be stronger than we are, but that we should confess our weakness and accept His strength. For God has provided all things for us in great abundance. Nothing is wanting but our will. If we are in a low position and short of sight, He has sent forth His light and His truth to lead and guide us. If we are weak of will, He sends His grace to strengthen and lift up our will. If we are uncertain of His ways, He has sent in our likeness His

Surrender your will to God

Son, who has ordained His Church for every place and time, to teach us His ways, that His truth and will may be always at our door. Our will may be weak, very weak; He asks for that will so that He may make it strong. All that God asks of us is our will; when we give to Him, in whatever condition, He will make it good. But, without our will, every provision to help and strengthen us is in vain; they cannot be ours.

Seek perfection

When virtue in all its perfection appeared in visible form to the eyes of men, when Christ, "the wisdom of God and the power of God,"[1] was seen, and heard, and touched by men, the humble alone were drawn to Him with wondering love. The sensual and the proud scorned and crucified Him. Something more than human eyes is required to love that virtue which descends from God. We cannot love that of which there is no element within us; and as the divine grace is the principle of Christian virtue, we first require the grace of humility to open our eyes to the divine beauty of that virtue which alone is worthy of God.

Christian virtue differs so widely from natural virtue that its power begins from God. The effect of virtue is

[1] 1 Cor. 1:24.

11

Patience and Humility

to make the person good, as well as his work, and to
perfect the soul according to the quality and degree of
the virtue exercised. Virtue, then, is not a sentiment or
a feeling, or any conscious enjoyment of one's own goodness, as some people are blind enough to imagine; the
pleasure of virtue is derived from its object and is a result of its exercise, while the reward of Christian virtue
is neither the virtue itself nor the enjoyment of it, but
the God of virtue. As St. Ambrose[2] says: "He who quits
himself and cleaves to virtue, loses his own and gains
what is eternal."

∞

The exercise of every habit of virtue includes the
following five distinct elements: the object of the virtue, the motive, the law of the virtue, the decision, and
the action.

The *object* of a virtue is that upon which, or toward
which, it is exercised. The object of faith, for example,
is the invisible truth revealed to us by God.

[2] Saint Ambrose (c. 339-397), Bishop of Milan and Doctor of the Church.

Seek perfection

The *motive* is the end we have in view. If a man helps the poor because it becomes his station in life, or because he accounts it honorable that no one in distress should leave his door unrelieved, this man has no higher motive or end to his virtue than his own honor, which is the heathen virtue of self-respect, beginning and ending in the man himself. If another assists the poor from the natural feeling of sympathy and kindliness, and looks to no higher motive, this is the natural virtue of benevolence, but nothing beyond. If the Christian helps the helpless not merely from kindliness but from the love of God, the motive is charity; and while his object is to help his suffering neighbor, his final motive is the love of God. "A work is then truly excellent," says St. Augustine,[3] "when the intention of the workman is struck out from the love of God, and returns again and again to rest in charity."

What a prodigious waste of value is caused to the virtues by exercising them on low motives and with low intentions, when they might be exercised on the very highest motives! The higher the motive, the nearer the

[3] Saint Augustine (354-430), Bishop of Hippo and Doctor of the Church.

soul is carried toward God, and this is true even in the lowest occupations.

Man sees in the face, but God in the heart. Man looks to the present value of the virtues as they affect this life, but God looks at the inward motive and intention as it regards eternity. The soul may draw near to God while the body is humbled down to the lowest toil; but this the world cannot see. There is a sublimity arising from the high flight of the intention above the meanness of the work — while both unite in the will of the workman — which angels may admire, but which the world, which sees but the mean work, can never understand. The poor man, rich in faith, who toils for the love of God and is generous with the little fruit of his labors, is much nearer to Heaven than the rich man who spends a fortune in good works from no higher motive than his natural inclination to benevolence.

Restlessness and excitement betray weakness; tranquillity is a quality that belongs to solid virtue.

The Christian virtues are the feet and wings whereby the soul moves in the direction of its final end; for even those duties that have their immediate end in this life, when directed by spiritual motives have their final end in God.

Seek perfection

∞

Our share in the world's affairs is too apt to take us from ourselves and from the divine exemplars seated in the inward man, and so bring us down from supernatural to natural habits, and from divine to human motives. It is, therefore, a great advancement in the virtues when the soul can be as simple, as sincere, as little given to vanity and as well habited in Christian goodness abroad in the world as at home. This depends much upon interior watchfulness and the keeping of the center of the soul in a state of calm recollectedness.

It belongs to the man who is in quest of his supreme good to draw as near to divine things as his condition of life will allow. To this we are often urged in the Gospel. Our Lord says: "Seek first the kingdom of God and His justice, and all these things shall be added to you."[4] And, again, He tells us: "Be ye perfect as your heavenly Father is perfect."[5] That is to say, as your heavenly Father is perfect God, be you perfect man, formed upon the type of the one perfect man.

[4] Matt. 6:33.
[5] Matt. 5:48.

Eradicate your bad habits

The two fundamental efforts of Christian virtue are these: the first is to leave our own selfish affections as much as we can, and to get as near to God with our will and affections as we may; the second is to develop the habit of acting as much on principle and as little on sentimentality as we can.

The whole labor of virtue consists in transferring the will from the attractions of nature to the attractions of grace, and in getting out of that narrow selfishness and away from those morbid sensibilities, to reach the divine atmosphere of truth and justice.

The only insurmountable obstacle is want of humility, to obtain which is the greatest labor of the soul.

There are several main reasons for the laboriousness of the first steps toward divine virtue and every great step thereafter. They demand self-renunciation and self-denial; they involve the breaking up of old and cherished habits to which nature clings; they require an ever-increasing humility descending further and further into the soul, pulling down the last remains of the pride of life and opening the innermost soul to the influence of grace; they have to master human respect; they have to detach the will from self-love, a detachment that rends nature to its center before the healing and restoring life of charity can enter thus far and close the wound of nature; and they have to transfer our powers more completely from nature to grace, and to raise what still acts in us under human motives to divine motives. All of this requires that we be subject to trials.

∞

The difficulties to be overcome in these ascensions to better things are not in them, but in ourselves, and there is a grandeur in the enterprise — a magnificence in the venture — that is full of encouragement.

What a charm it is to be linked and united more closely and ever more closely with the eternal mysteries! What a help in the divine power! What a glory it is for us mortals to be always approaching nearer and nearer to the supreme and infinite Good! What are all the petty interests of this mortal life, that they should absorb the soul, compared with the wonderful things above us that hang on the tree of life, and that are always ready for the souls that are willing to reach up to them.

We have also a divine leader, not in the remote distance of history, but with us, always with us: God in our nature, God with us,[6] God within us; our way, truth, and life,[7] lighting us to the virtues, and giving us the force to practice them.

Nothing cramps the freedom of the soul in a greater degree than the fear of what others will think and say. The first thing to be done after taking the narrow way is to shut the world out of consideration and look only to the approval of God.

The burden of life is from ourselves; its lightness from the grace of Christ and the love of God.

[6] Matt. 1:23.
[7] Cf. John 14:6.

Patience and Humility

∞

Charity gives peace to the soul. For whoever loves God above all things rests his heart on the eternal peace. "God is greater than our heart."[8] He can fill all our desires, and when the heart knows this, the nearer it draws to the Divine Fountain of Good, the more it finds repose. But we must keep in mind that charity can never come from oneself; it can only come from God.

∞

Let it be plainly understood that we cannot return to God unless we enter first into ourselves. God is everywhere, but He is not everywhere to us. There is but one point in the universe where God communicates with us, and that is the center of our own soul. There He waits for us; there He meets us; there He speaks to us. To seek Him, therefore, we must enter into our own interior.

[8] 1 John 3:20.

Humility

Recognize God's gifts

There are four virtues, the fruits of divine grace, which in their union bring the soul to God: humility, faith, purity, and charity. With the loss of the knowledge of the true God they were lost to the world, and our Lord Jesus Christ brought them down anew from Heaven to mankind. Their union in the soul is the distinctive sign of Christian holiness.

When pride throws off obedience to God, humility dies. When the mind rebels against the authority of God as the revealer of truth, faith dies together with humility. When the graceless soul allows the body to revolt and defile the soul with uncleanness, holiness is extinct. When self-love holds the place of charity, the spiritual life of man is no more. When these virtues have departed, the man is left to nature and the world, but to nature in cruel disorder, and to the world, not as

Patience and Humility

God has made it in His goodness, but as man has made it in his concupiscence; to the world as it is taken up for a final end in place of God.

The men of the world have their measure of virtue, but that virtue falls short of God, and ends in this life. They measure their virtues upon the requirements of their fellowmen.

∞

The least known among the virtues, and consequently the most misunderstood, is the virtue of humility, and yet it is the very groundwork of the Christian religion.

Humility is a grace of the soul that cannot be expressed in words, and is known only by experience. It is an unspeakable treasure of God, and can only be called the gift of God. "Learn," He said — not from angels, not from men, not from books — but learn from my presence, light, and action within you, "that I am meek and humble of heart, and you shall find rest to your souls."[9] The more we are subject to God, the nearer we

[9] Cf. Matt. 11:29.

are to Him. He is infinitely above us, but by this very subjection we ascend to Him, and find in Him whatever is truly great.

∞

Humility consists in the confession of the grace of God. The first office of the grace of God is to make us sensible of the giver.

The grand object for which we came into existence is more than the light and grace of God; it is God Himself, and those gifts are given to guide and lead and help us to Him. We are not our own God, nor are the things around or beneath us our God, however useful in their place and order, but God is our God, and whatever comes from God that is better than ourselves helps us grow closer to Him. We have but the capacity for God, and the power of working with the good we receive. Pride is the practical denial of this truth, a truth that springs from the constitution of our nature. And therefore it is said in Holy Scripture that "pride was not made for man."[10]

[10]Ecclus. 10:22.

Patience and Humility

∞

Again, humility is the interior, spiritual, sacrificial action through which, with the profoundest veneration and gratitude, we offer to God the being and life we have received from Him, with the desire and prayer that we may die to ourselves and live to Him; that we may be wholly changed and transformed into His likeness, detached from earth and united with God. But as we come to our God from sin and dark ingratitude, we owe more to Him than our being and our life; we owe Him the contrition, the breaking to pieces of our sinful form, with regret and sorrow that we have defiled and defaced His beautiful work; we owe to Him to throw away every breath of vanity, falsehood, and evil, which, when cast out of us, is nothing.

∞

Perfect humility is the fruit of perfect charity. The more we love God, the less we value ourselves. He who is truly humble, truly empty of himself, is a vessel of election to God, full to overflowing with His benedictions. He has only to ask to receive still more. He is the child of all the Beatitudes: poor in spirit, meek of heart, and hungering and thirsting for justice.[11]

When humility finds nothing in itself to rest upon, it finds its true center, and that center is God. For the humble soul alone has got the divine as well as the human measure of things.

[11]Cf. Matt. 5:3-11.

Base your humility
on twelve foundations

The first ground of humility is our creation from nothing. We are of a short time; our beginning was feeble, as became our origin, and nothing was the womb of us all. Whence are we? From the creative will of God. What are we? An existence dependent on the will of God. Where are we going? Onwards, ever onwards — the body to the dust, the soul to the judgment seat of God.

God is the one, absolute, perfect being; we are but existences, the products of His will, dependent on Him for all we are and have; and all this great scene about us that fills our senses is of less value than the last soul that was created and born into this world. For the soul is for God, but this visible universe for the service and probation of the soul.

Patience and Humility

The second ground of humility is our intellectual light. That light makes us reasonable creatures. In that light, we see the first principles of truth, order, and justice; it is the foundation of our mind and of our conscience. Man is variable and changeable, and one man differs from another; but the light of truth and justice shines one and the same to all, and the chief difference between one man and another is in the degree of his communion with that light.

∞

The third ground of humility is in our dependence on the Providence of God. Our life with all its conditions is in the hand of God.

The fourth ground of humility is in our sins; by them we have deformed and denaturalized our nature, ungraced ourselves before God, and incurred His reprobation.

The fifth ground of humility is in the weakness, the ignorance, and the concupiscence that we have inherited from Original Sin, and have increased by our actual sins.

The sixth ground of humility is in the open perils and hidden snares with which we are surrounded. Error in all its forms, and unbelief in all its modes and varieties move in their motley shapes through nearly every grade of life, with the apparent unconsciousness that truth is one and comes from God. The widespread evil of modern life is the amazing indifference to the well-being of the soul. An intense activity outside the soul pursues its many ways in the name of progress, although the object or ultimate aim of that progress is neither thought of nor spoken of. It is chiefly a progress, not to, but from the soul; not to, but from God.

The seventh ground of humility is in the special odiousness and deformity of pride, which is in direct opposition, beyond every other vice, to the order, reason, and truth of things. Pride turns all things from God; humility turns all things to God.

The eighth ground of humility is in the consideration of what this virtue does for us. It opens the soul to the truth of Christ, and opens the heart to the grace of Christ.

The ninth ground of humility is the knowledge of God and His divine perfections.

The tenth ground of humility is the secure rest provided for the soul in the unspeakable benefits of our divine Redeemer.

Patience and Humility

The eleventh ground of humility is in our distance in this vale of suffering and tears from the supreme object of our soul, and the risks we run in the meanwhile from our infirmities.

The twelfth ground of humility is the holy fear of the judgments of God. For unless we shelter ourselves well in the humility of Christ, and do penance, and use the world as though we used it not, we are not safe. Unless, again, a humble dependence on God is the foundation of our life, and the love of God is our ruling affection, we know not in what state God will find us in the hour when we shall pass from this world.

Look for the good in others

If the virtue of humility is often misunderstood when directly exercised toward God, the same virtue is liable to still greater misconception when exercised toward our neighbor. There are two things to be considered in every man, and these two things have to be well and carefully distinguished from each other: what the man is of himself, and what he is by the superadded gifts of God. Every man should subject what is purely his own to what is of God, whether that which is of God is in himself or in another.

This is the principle of humility in its exercise toward our neighbor; it is not a reverence given to human nature, but to the gifts of God within that nature.

But the same humility forbids the unreasonableness of judging another man's soul. We can act only on what we know, and we always know much more of our own internal weakness and defects than we can know in the case of another person.

Few persons, perhaps, reflect on the beauty of the reward we receive for humility to our neighbor. This humility opens the soul to all the good that God has planted in other souls.

Those are the happy, sunshiny souls that are open to see all the good influences of God around them, and that receive into themselves the reflection of the divine good which God has given to other souls. This is one of the great privileges of a truly religious society where humility and charity are the dominant virtues: each soul is always receiving a beautiful and powerful influence from all the rest of the community.

The very spectacle gives a light to the words of our Lord, that "where two or three are gathered together in my name, there I am in the midst of them."[12]

∞

It is the will of men acting apart from God, and preferring in their pride to see the evil rather than the

[12]Matt. 18:20.

good in their fellowmen, that so bitterly entangles this world of human nature. It is the myriads of self-wills, each impelled by its own self-love, that produce the knots, the ravels, and the interminable complications that make this world such a wearying perplexity to those thoughtful minds devoid of the wisdom that descends from God. Even David was perplexed in his musings on these things until he remembered the judgments of God.

The tragedy of human life is not the strife of free will with fate that the ignorant pagans imagined, but the collision of pride with the providence of humiliation; of self-will, destined always to defeat, against the will of God.

There is such an enormous distance between what we are by nature and what God would have us be by grace, so that we may pass from misery to happiness; and the obstacles within us that hold us back or throw us the other way are of such a kind — tending to seek false instead of true greatness, in the exaltation of ourselves, and not in ascending to things greater than ourselves — that this alone shows us what a great part humility must take in replacing us on the path that leads to God.

Patience and Humility

Although the light that descends to us from God is the chief principle of self-knowledge, the watching of our conduct toward our neighbors also helps us very much to know ourselves.

Trust in the Father's tender love

Although all the virtues imitate God, God Himself has not our virtues, but He is one infinite virtue and perfection. Our virtue is a struggle against frailty, a progress to better things, and a triumph over weakness; and it is perfected, as St. Paul says, amid infirmity. It is the effect of good will, helped by the grace of God, to bring us near to God.

∞

The Father gives all He has to every creature He has made, and to His intelligent creatures, capable and willing to receive them, He gives things divine as well as earthly; but with them He gives the law of justice, which demands that we give them all back to Him. To do this is humility in man.

Patience and Humility

Humility, therefore, is nothing less than the reflection in our life of the truth and justice of God. By humility we also imitate the purity of God.

∞

What, then, is the benignity of God but the lowering and diminishing of Himself in the minds and hearts of His rational creatures, so that He may adapt Himself to our limited understanding and contracted sense?

God descends into our ways to raise us to His divine ways, and we obtain the divine likeness to the degree in which we love Him. God delights to call Himself our Father, and by that holy title He seems to preside over His human family in a homely and familiar way. It is unspeakable what service God is always rendering to us, and what benignity and condescension we are daily and hourly receiving from our heavenly Father.

The humble ways of God in this world are His tender, loving ways. They are the sublimest of all lessons to the proud, if the proud could only learn them. But while they attract the humble, and fill their souls with sweetness, proving, above all else, the love which God has for them, they repel the proud, who could not receive them without the utter condemnation of their own evil condition.

∞

Had we the true spirit of God, and a humble trust in His benignant care of all humble things that do His will, we should never lack anything that might conduce to our eternal good. For His special love and care is for the humble, whose sincere spirit resembles His own.

All the examples of divine condescension that we can accumulate cannot bring home to the truly humble soul a conviction equal to the loving sense within that soul of what God is to the humble. If He rejects the proud, it is because they are alien to His nature; if He receives the humble, it is because they are conformable to His life.

Those humble spirits who look to nothing but His goodness are His true children, and He loves to yield to their prayers and expostulations. God loves to be resisted in His displeasure, and to be restrained by the humble from inflicting punishment. One saint will often save a nation; so true is it that humble souls are the

Patience and Humility

hinges on which God moves the world. Humility so perfects man for God that when the Son of God took our nature, He could find no other virtue so capable of uniting that nature with God.

Follow Christ's example of humility

The scriptural sense of the word *master* signifies one who teaches with authority. This title was given to the Son of God both by His disciples and His adversaries.

Who is the true Master but He who is all that He teaches and incomparably more than He teaches? Jesus Christ was the substantive master of humility.

When we speak of Christ as the master of humility, we speak of something preeminently great and excelling. The Son of God could not take the nature of man without making that nature morally perfect, and He has shown in Himself that the foundation of moral perfection in a creature is perfect humility.

He could not, again, take the offices of our Mediator and Redeemer upon Him without showing us in a preeminent way by what virtue we are reconciled to God and made open to His sanctifying gifts. This virtue

Patience and Humility

He therefore manifested the most conspicuously in Himself. He took it as His singular prerogative because it was the perfect subjection of His humanity to His divinity, because it was the virtue by which He redeemed the world, and because it is the one virtue by which every soul that He came to redeem returns to God. To this virtue, therefore, as to His great human prerogative, He especially appealed as to the chief lesson that we are to learn of Him, "Learn of me, for I am meek and humble of heart."[13]

∞

The Son of God could never have accepted this condition of humility but for the most divine reason of glorifying the Holy Trinity, which He did in taking the headship of humanity, in perfecting that humanity in Himself, in recovering that humanity to God when lost, and in restoring that humanity to the great and divine end for which every intelligent soul was created. He took this humble condition to drive back and destroy the huge invasion of pride that was the ruin of the

[13]Matt. 11:29.

human race. "Being in the form of God, He thought it no robbery to be equal with God, but emptied Himself, taking the form of a servant, being made in the likeness of man; and in habit found as a man, He humbled Himself, becoming obedient unto death, even the death of the cross."[14] In which form of a servant He was less than the Father, less than Himself, unequal to Himself, unlike Himself, and emptied to all appearance of Himself, in this land of misery and sorrow, that by restoring us to humility He might restore us to God.

Thus through His Incarnation the Son of God both consecrated and deified humility, making it more glorious to be humble with God, than to be exalted with pride among the children of men. To imitate Christ in His humility is something truly great.

But pride was not the only evil that withheld men from God; the covetousness of the things of this world, and the appetite for sensual pleasures drew them with an overpowering fascination from the knowledge of

[14]Phil. 2:6-8.

Patience and Humility

God and from the love of eternal good. On this account it was necessary that we should have the example not only of humility but also of self-abnegation, which is so intimately connected with humility.

Our Lord, therefore, united His humility with poverty, and His poverty with self-abnegation. And this was not merely for our example, but because the life of humility, poverty, and self-abnegation is the most perfect of human lives, as depending on God alone, and as setting the things of this mortal life at their true value as compared with the things of eternity. Yet through all the humility and poverty of Christ, His divinity shines, as in the humility of His saints, the Spirit of God shines through every abasement.

∞

The calm and gentle way in which the Son of God first makes Himself known to the people of Nazareth — to those who had known Him for thirty years from His infancy — and lets them know that He, whom they had known only as an obedient son and a pious working man, was the expected Messiah and the fulfillment of the prophets, has always appeared to me to be one of the most remarkable passages in the history of His divine life.

It is remarkable not only for the calm gentleness of His bearing at so solemn a moment, but for the humility with which He makes an announcement so startling to His audience. There is none of the excitement or fervor of enthusiasm with which mere human nature would have announced a great personal claim for the first time, especially when contrary to all the preconceptions of his hearers; there is the calmness of God in the figure and voice of man. He reads the prophetic description of His divine mission in the ordinary course of His duty as a reader in the Synagogue, and then, when all eyes are fixed upon Him, He gently drops the word to their attentive ears, "This day is fulfilled this Scripture in your ears."[15] All the rest He leaves to the silent inference of their own minds.

Let it be further observed that in all His humble words and ways, our divine Lord never speaks directly

[15]Luke 4:21.

of His own humility but once. He lives and breathes and personifies the virtue, as what is inseparable from Him; but of His own humility He spoke but once. He spoke once because that was necessary for our instruction; He spoke once to consecrate this wonderful virtue; He spoke only once because of the exceeding delicacy and hidden nature of the virtue, which, like purity, is far too modest to be spoken of by its possessor except in a case of absolute necessity. And in this, also, He conveys to us a profound instruction.

"Come," He says, "to me, learn of me"; "I am the way, the truth, and the life: no man cometh to the Father except through me."[16] He is the way to Heaven, the truth from Heaven, the life that brings Heaven. He says, "Come to me; learn this one thing from me, and you shall know all things; learn this one thing from me, and you shall possess all things; learn to be meek and humble of heart." There is nothing so wonderful in power as the humility of Christ, who, resting the created nature of His humanity wholly upon His Divine nature, ascribes nothing whatever to that human nature, which He knew so perfectly to be nothing without God.

[16]Cf. Matt. 11:28, 29; John 14:6.

Follow Christ's example of humility

Having once learned from Christ that the great lesson He has come to teach us is His own meekness and humility, we then discover that His Incarnation, His birth, all the actions of His life, His sufferings and death, all speak to us, and breathe into us, this divine lesson of humility; and everywhere, even when His voice is silent, His life and conduct say to us: "Learn of me, because I am meek and humble of heart."

The Passion of our Lord presents all the great virtues in their perfection for our imitation, whether self-denial, poverty of spirit, obedience, silence, humility, purity, patience, prayer, resignation, contempt of the world, or charity. But among all these virtues, He preeminently appears as the master of humility. His Passion is the book of humility; His Cross is the throne of humility; the terrible way from the Mount of Olives to Mount Calvary is the substantive exposition of the words "Learn of me, for I am meek and humble of heart." The Cross is the instrument of contrition upon which the earthly man is broken to be reformed into the heavenly man. The Cross is the divine school of patience,

Patience and Humility

the school of self-abnegation, the school of penance, and the school of charity. The foot of the Cross, where Mary stood with John, and where the prostrate Magdalene wept her loving grief, is the great school of humility, where the soul is purified and brought to God. There forever sounds the great command of the divine Master, "Learn of me, for I am meek and humble of heart."

Empty your soul of self

It is impossible to imagine holiness in any of God's creatures without humility and purity. For as chastity is the body's purity, humility is the soul's purity, and purity is the first condition of sanctity. The more humble and pure a soul is, the more it looks away from itself into the perfect type of holiness in whose light it sees nothing in itself but the gifts of God and its own defects.

Humility is the virtue that measures our failures from justice, and our distance from the eternal justice, and that labors to make and to keep us truthful and honest within ourselves and before God. What God seeks in man, what He loves in man, and what He rewards in man is humility.

Patience and Humility

∞

St. Paul calls the true Christian God's building and God's husbandry.[17] He lays in us the foundation of faith that we may know Him, of hope that we may desire Him, and of charity that we may love Him, serve Him, and rejoice in Him. But this can be done only in a soul duly disposed. For God cannot build a divine edifice on an earthly foundation, or upon self-love, or upon self-elation, or upon self-seeking, or upon hollow, delusive, revolting pride, or upon animal concupiscence. A building upon such quicksand would soon be swallowed up.

All of this creation of our own, if anything so vain ought to be called a creation, must be swept away. And why? So that God may find His own creation, and not a mere falsified creature made into a lie by vanity and pride, but His own creature as He made it, pure and simple, and duly subject to Him, that He may work what is good and holy on His own foundation.

We are not created with virtue, but with nature; we are not created with grace; that must be given to our nature.

[17]Cf. 1 Cor. 3:9.

∞

"Empty yourself, and see that I am God."[18] Humility is the animated capacity of the soul, vacated of self-seeking, and looking to God with desire to be filled with His light, grace, and goodness. God will not throw away His noble gifts upon those who cannot be made worthy of them, even by the gifts themselves. If the soul is not subject to God, as well as open, it cannot receive the grace of the Christian virtues.

Frail as man is, humility will make a foundation in him strong enough for God to raise an edifice upon it that shall last for eternity. The progress of humility is the progress of the soul. We may know the extent of the grace that is given to us by the strength of our humility. Our very perfection is humility. The gifts and prerogatives conferred on the Blessed Virgin were all given to her humility; this she expressly declares in her canticle of gratitude.[19]

[18]Cf. Ps. 45:11 (RSV = Ps. 46:10).
[19]Luke 1:46-55.

Treasure God above all

Christian magnanimity is a most generous virtue, be-cause it is essentially opposed to selfish considerations. It is greatness of soul opposed to littleness of soul. It is also concerned with security or tranquillity, which rests with a sincere conscience on God.

Great generosity gives to every virtue the quality of magnanimity, because generosity proceeds from great-ness of soul, great in aiming to please God, and to do Him honor. The sons and daughters of the eternal King ought to have great souls; they ought to be ready to do great things for His honor and glory.

He is magnanimous who forcefully mortifies his senses, giving no more to the body than it needs, that the spirit may hold command, and be free, and the soul be filled with good things. He is magnanimous who will not let his soul be ruled by offensive words or violent deeds. He is great-minded who has his chief conversation with the eternal truth and justice. Why should that truth be always near us, and we commonly far away, unless from our little-mindedness? He is great-minded who keeps himself in the divine Presence, and who is never long away from the sense of the eternal God. God is always with us; why should we not always be with God? The great souls of all ages have walked with God.

Soft and pusillanimous souls are too weak to walk steadfastly before God through the pilgrimage of life; but the great-souled are subject from their inmost heart to God, accounting that nothing can be greater for them than to be in the hands of God. The great-souled are full of faith — a faith that so lights up the eternal world to them, that the mortal things of this world fade before their eyes like dying flowers. The great-souled are magnanimous in sacrificing the love of self to the love of God, until all their strength flows into charity. Happy are they who are released from bondage to themselves, that they may be large and free in the generous atmosphere of light and grace. All that we require is that the soul be open and generous. Humility opens the soul; charity makes it generous.

Treasure God above all

∞

For nearly two thousand years, the world has known the Son of God in human nature.

Christ Jesus was the perfect man in perfect union with God, the model of manhood to all men, most perfect in magnanimity as in all virtues, yet the world could not understand Him; so very different is the divine from the human view of magnanimity.

Although both heathen and Christian magnanimity aim at making the soul great, and do this by seeking great things and despising little things, there is an immeasurable distance between them that is still visible in the man of the world as compared with the servant of Christ. The man who prefers himself to God, or the things of this world to the things of God, or the interests of time to the interests of eternity, or being honored by men to being honored by God, is not great-souled, but little-souled.

The sublime way of humility is that a man be poor in himself and rich in God.

Resist pride

As pride is the root of all evil, the vice of vices, and the destruction of the virtues, it is the chief enemy of God and of man. It contradicts the whole reason of humility. It is not only irrational, as all sins are, but it is also an uncreaturely sin, which other sins are not.

The proud man does not behave like one whom God has recently created from nothing, and whom He may summon to His presence at any hour. He acts as though he were not dependent on God, and as if what he is, and has, were not altogether owing to the divine will and bounty. This vice is so thoroughly opposed to the nature and condition of man, as well as to the rights and claims of God, and is so destructive of all spiritual good, that God has proclaimed to us this warning in His Scripture, "Pride was not made for man."[20]

The greatness of the soul is its capacity for God. A soul without the Spirit of God is an existence without its object, a mere failure from the reason of its existence, like a house that is never inhabited, or a body that is never animated. The soul can be perfected, as the very constitution of its nature is an image of God, only insofar as it possesses the life of God.

Sin is an aversion from God and a conversion to the creature, accepted as a good in place of God against all reason and justice; and pride is the aversion from God in all sin.

Inordinate self-love is the cause of pride.

∞

From the beginning to the end of the Holy Scriptures, we shall find, if we study them attentively, one fundamental truth, and one unceasing admonition. We hear it in the Garden of Eden; we see it on the Cross. It runs through the sacred histories, is loud in the prophets,

[20]Ecclus. 10:22.

frequent in the books of wisdom, continuous in the Gospels, and rises in many pages of the apostolic writings. This fundamental truth instructs us to know, this constant admonition exhorts us to act on the belief, that what God accepts from man is humility, and that what He rejects is pride. His blessings are for the humble; His maledictions are for the proud. In every virtue, it is humility that He rewards; in every vice, it is pride that He punishes. And when we remember that it is humility that subjects the soul and the virtues to God, and that it is pride that sends the soul away from God, and inflames the vices with its malice, we shall see that it cannot be otherwise.

Let us, then, entreat God with all our power, that in His mercy He would deliver us from pride, and would grant us the inestimable gift of humility, that we may not follow the evil spirits in their pride to destruction, but Christ, the divine Master of humility, to sanctification. May God in His goodness grant us this now and forever. Amen.

Submit to God's authority

The light of reason is sufficient to teach the knowledge of God, but not to bring man into union with his Creator. For the light, naturally implanted in the human mind, bears witness to God, and the conscience is His voice. But the pride that is in man separates him from God, turns his soul from the light, corrupts his interior sense, and smites him with spiritual blindness.

In the Scriptures and the Church we learn that the true progress of man is toward God, and that the path of this progress is upward to greater truth and higher justice. But the heathen world teaches us the terrible lesson of the final end of false progress, of progress away from God through the dreary downward path by the ways of negation and false liberty. First, the sense of dependence on God is lost, and so the virtue of humility departs. Then man forgets his Creator, forgets Him until he no longer knows that he is a creature, and so the intellectual principle of humility disappears from his mind. Pride, then, remains master of his heart without a rival; but still wanting a god, although a god consistent with his license, he begins to deify the creature.

∞

The rejection of the humility of faith and of the gospel is rapidly bringing the world at large to the old heathen conditions of thought and conduct, and to the old heathen confusion of substituting the powers of the world for the sovereignty of God. This is manifested in many ways.

Again, the idolatries of the modern world are in various respects grosser than the idolatries of the ancient world. For the ancient world idealized nature and, however erroneously, still associated that nature with some ideal of the divine, and ascribed divine attributions to its departed heroes; but the modern idolatries are given to the gross, unidealized facts and products of nature, and to human inventions, without having associated any divine ideal with their powers. The ancient world had a sense of religion, however corruptly applied; but modern heathenism has dismissed every sense of the divine, and has given its devotion to the bare powers and phenomena of nature, or to the worship of poor fallen humanity; to the deification of accumulated wealth; to the veneration of mechanical inventions; to the cultivation of material luxury; and to the superexaltation of pride, independence, and self-reliance.

Whatever a man seeks, honors, or exalts more than God is the god of his idolatry. There is no need of temples, altars or statues for material, mental, or social idolatry; whatever is preferred in mind and heart to God, whatever is chosen as the chief end of man's pursuit in place of God, constitutes the idolatry of these times.

Modern states have certainly not claimed divinity for themselves like the old heathen government; their tendency is to discard religion as a foundation, and to remove its sanctions from beneath their constitutions and laws. Hence the ever-growing tendency to substitute temporary expediency for the fixed principles of wisdom, and the unstable voice of the multitude for the maxims of experience and the long foresight of prudence. There is everywhere visible an enormous jealousy of the authority of religion over the souls of men; and like the heathens of old, the ambition of states is to reign alone, and to have no power above their own in the world. In nothing is this shown more than in those secular systems of education held in the hands of the state, in which all minds shall be trained by compulsion upon the mind of the state, after the fashion of the Spartans, leaving the rights of God and of the family out of consideration, and reducing all minds to one dead level of rationalism.

Do not yield to vanity

Vanity, or vainglory, is the offspring of pride, that detestable vice. It is such a light, fond thing, that, if its seductions did not weaken and undermine the best-formed minds and hearts both of men and women, it would be unworthy of any serious consideration. A man or woman given up to vanity is filled with light follies unworthy of the dignity of the soul and the noble end for which the soul is created. It may be more secret, as a rule, in men than in women, but it is nonetheless dishonest for that reason.

The word *vanity* sounds of things hollow, shallow, and trifling; but it is no trifle that makes the soul light and trivial, and unrobes it of its dignity. Every creature has in it a natural vanity, because, created from nothing, and if not supported by God, it would of its own nature go back to nothingness. It is vain also, because by the mere force of its own nature no creature can come to its final end.

∽

The worst effect of vanity is that it makes the soul empty and inane. It not only destroys good but leads to evil. As nothing in human nature is so sensitive as vanity, there is nothing that suffers more. It is easily wounded, often mortified, and frequently disappointed. What vanity tempts is the empty soul, and the soul inflated with the ruinous pride of ambition. The remedy for this disorder is in the exercise of that most sincere of virtues which wars against pride and all its offspring, and which bears the name of holy humility.

Let humility increase your faith

Our life begins in utter ignorance of all things, and our mind is first opened by the instinctive faith that we place in those around us. Without this faith we could make no beginning of knowledge. The simple, open, confiding spirit of childhood enables us to learn much in a short time. But youth also advances in knowledge through faith in the teacher. We are now speaking of human faith. There are three moral elements in this teachableness. The first is the consciousness of ignorance, which is an element of natural humility. The second is the opening of the mind to the teacher, which is a second element of humility. The third is the belief given to the teacher, which is a third element of humility. This is the human way of knowledge; it begins with faith, and the greater part by far of everyone's knowledge has no other ground than faith.

Patience and Humility

∞

The principles of divine faith are totally different from the principles of human faith. Human faith rests on the testimony of man; divine faith on the testimony of God. The natural man cannot understand divine faith; he must be prepared for it, and God alone can prepare him. As the truth revealed by God is above all created nature, and is divine, the grace of God must dispose the soul for its reception. And this disposition is obtained not by study, but by prayer; not by disputation, but by humility.

Faith is the first light, the heralding light, the foundation placed in us of what in its final perfection will be the Beatific Vision of God. It is the beginning of the eternal ways in us, the commencement of our union with God, and is compared in the Scriptures to a first espousal of the soul with God: "I will espouse thee to me in faith."[21] Faith is the first thing that makes us acceptable to God, for as Paul says, "Without faith it is impossible to please God."[22] We please Him by the

[21]Osee 2:20 (RSV = Hos. 2:20).
[22]Heb. 11:6.

Let humility increase your faith

humility with which we acknowledge Him to be the fountain of truth and subject ourselves to Him as the children of His truth.

∞

Faith is by its very nature a subjection of the mind and will to God as He is the sovereign truth, a subjection to His divine authority as the illuminator and teacher of the soul, and a subjection to the truth which He teaches by revealing. Moreover, as a test and trial of this subjection to Him, God is pleased to require that this subjection of faith shall be openly made and manifested before all men, by our open submission to the Church which He has appointed to represent His authority, to the voice of Her teaching, and to Her ministry of grace, as exercised in His name and by His power.

This is not only faith, but the humility of faith, because it is the subjection of the mind and heart to the authority of God and to His truth, in the way that He imposes and prescribes.

Humility must remove pride and open the soul so that the grace of faith may enter.

Patience and Humility

∞

What prevented such numbers of those who followed our divine Lord and, attracted by curiosity, heard His words and saw His mighty power in His miracles, from believing in Him? Our Lord Himself has proclaimed the three causes of their unbelief: their pride, their love of this world's interests, and their human respect. And He proclaimed the two conditions which would alone enable them to follow Him as disciples, and to become members of His kingdom. These were humility and self-abnegation.

Humility, then, is the groundwork of faith, and faith is the groundwork of the other Christian virtues, which are all exercised in the light of faith. Humility frees the soul from pride and error; faith fills it with light and truth. Humility opens the soul so that faith may enter.

Humility brings us to the knowledge of ourselves, and faith to the knowledge of God. But the knowledge of God brings so great an increase to the knowledge of ourselves, when we use that knowledge rightly, that humility may be said to rest on faith as much as faith rests on humility.

Let humility increase your faith

The force and wisdom of faith is the love of God and our neighbor. For charity is the light of faith, and faith is the light of charity. Wherefore let us cultivate humility, that we may have a larger soul for faith and charity; and faith, that we may have a greater light from God and deeper knowledge of the eternal mysteries; and charity, that we may obtain the fruit of faith and humility through the closer union of our soul with God. But faith is cultivated by prayer, by meditation, by contemplation, and by living, thinking, and acting in the light of faith, and in the presence of God.

School yourself in humility

Every science is founded upon certain fixed and un-changeable principles of truth, and is guided by rules that spring from those principles. The science of humility rests upon the knowledge of God and of oneself; it fills the whole distance between the creature and the Creator. The giver of this science is God, whose light descends into our interior, and shows us what we are in His sight, and what we ought to be.

Hence the science of humility is profound, descending as well as ascending beyond the sphere of human comprehension; for the depths of the soul are unfathomable, and the heights of God are unattainable in this time of probation. We must, therefore, learn the great laws of humility from God, who has sent us His Son to teach them; He Himself is their great example, and His Cross is lifted up as the beacon-flame of His doctrine over the whole troubled sea of human life. There is one unrivaled master in every science, and our Lord Jesus Christ is the supreme master of humility.

But the science of humility is not humility; the science provides only the knowledge and the rules for its exercise. Humility is a virtue and belongs to practice; it is a divine art and discipline exercised in the deeper regions of the soul. By this discipline the soul is opened, enlightened, purified, and invigorated to act with freedom in the gifts of God.

The rules that guide the science of humility spring from all the relations that ought in justice to exist between the soul and God.

The Church has Her great schools of humility in Her monastic and religious institutions. They may be properly called the schools of the Beatitudes, devoted as they are to the methodical cultivation of the divine counsels that were delivered to mankind by the Son of God. They are founded on the virtues of humility and charity; their system of training is based upon humility; and their discipline is perfected in the exercise of that virtue, whose spirit pervades the Beatitudes — as it begins with the first of them — and whose true disciples are the choice and privileged portion of the Church of God.

Grow in love of God and neighbor through humility

Let us ascend in mind through the grace of God to the divine fountain of all charity. God is charity;[23] charity is the life and perfection of His being. What an infinitude of life and love is expressed in these three little words: God is charity!

As the seashell on the sandy shore cannot contain the ocean that rolls around the world; as the laboring breast of man cannot contain the pure and boundless ether that fills the heavens; as the body of man could not pass into the intense conflagration of the sun without instant destruction; neither can the soul of man embrace, comprehend, or enter into the infinite charity of God.

[23] 1 John 4:8.

Patience and Humility

Yet some drops of the ocean are in the shell; some little modified breath of that ether is in the breast of man; and some tempered rays of the warmth of that sun are in our earthly frame. God has also deigned to impart to the soul of the humble Christian some created rays from His uncreated charity, which are full of divine life and love; and in virtue of that sublime gift, the moment the words "God is charity" are sounded in his ears, he knows and feels to his inmost core that it is so.

∞

There is no other reason for the existence of this world than the charity of God and the communication of His charity. The world was made for man, man for the soul, and the soul for charity; and charity unites the soul with God. From charity God created the world, and by charity He perfects the end for which the world was made, for that end is the happiness of souls possessed of charity. There is a kind of life in the soul without charity, but it is not the life for which the soul was made; not true life, but initiatory and merely infantile life, which is life in pain and sorrow from want of our true life.

Grow in love of God and neighbor

∞

Humility disposes the soul and prepares the way for charity, and greater humility prepares and disposes the soul for greater charity. True humility never was, never is, and never can be without charity. Humility is the sacrificial element in all sincere love. For as love is the transfer of our affection from ourselves to another, it includes a surrender of self-love, and this surrender is humility. But when we give up our love from ourselves to God, this giving up of our love of self to God is humility, and the love that we give to God is charity.

To humble souls — for they alone are capable — the grace of charity will never be wanting; for the God who is charity does not mock His children, but when He commands them to love Him with their whole heart and soul and strength and mind,[24] He gives them the charity by which they may love Him.

True charity to our neighbor is to love him, whether friend or foe, as we love ourselves, in God, unto God, and for God's sake. For the charitable love of our neighbor is embraced in the love of God, proceeds from the

[24]Cf. Matt. 22:37; Mark 12:30; Luke 10:27.

love of God, and ends in the love of God. Nothing makes us more like to God than to forgive those who offend and injure us; and we may certainly obtain more grace and glory from God through persecution than through kindness, if we know how to use it rightly. Of this true test of charity our Lord gave us the example in His conduct to the traitor Judas.

Charity is the way to man as well as to God. It conciliates all intelligences. And although there may be much excitement in what the world calls pleasure, there is no solid joy of life or peace of heart except in charity. "He who abideth in charity, abideth in God, and God in him."[25]

---

[25] 1 John 4:16.

Patience

Strengthen your soul
through patience

The perfection of the Christian soul consists in that complete and exquisite charity whereby we love God above all things, and our neighbor as ourselves, for the love of God. This love, this charity that perfects the soul, is the sublimest gift that we can receive from God in this our exile, because God Himself is charity, and the life of God is charity. By charity God lives in us and we in Him.

The love of God is our spiritual life; it makes the will, the affections, the soul, and the work of the soul good. Without the charity of God we are nothing. Woe, then, to that false science which puts matter before spirit, sense before conscience, darkness before light, and creature before God, and professes to find the cause of light and love, those sublimest gifts of the eternal charity of God, in the lowest and least spiritual elements of His creation. It is an awful proof of the extent to which cultivated intellects, lost to charity, can be won over by pride, and of the utter perversion of that light of intelligence which their minds have received from God.

∞

The grace of patience is given with the grace of charity, as well to protect it as to bring it to perfection. True patience for the love of God is therefore the highest test and most evident proof of the presence of a noble degree of charity, because it can be obtained, even with the help of grace, only by dint of labor, self-combat, and effort; but we have the sensible result in the possession of oneself and in peace of soul.

The soul cannot possess itself when it is held in the possession of its mortal senses, appetites, or passions, or when held in bondage to creatures that are less than itself and that trouble, degrade, and divide the soul, and distract its mind and will from what is greater and better than itself. It can only possess itself in God through charity and patience: in charity, adhering to God; in patience, persevering in that adherence despite all the perturbations and fears of its inferior nature.

∞

So intimate is the connection between patience and humility, that neither of these virtues can make much progress without the other; nor can charity advance toward its perfection without their aid.

To the spiritual man, patience is more essential than food, for food strengthens the body and preserves it from weakness, but patience fortifies the soul, and without it no virtue can be firm and solid. But as we are obliged to take more care of the soul than of the body, it is evident that we ought to be more solicitous for patience than for food.

God is our patience, our fortitude, and our strength, provided we rest our souls on Him, adhere to Him, are subject to His strengthening influences, and work with them in loyal cooperation.

Patience is the medicine of our enfeebled nature; it fortifies the will, soothes the irritabilities that derange the soul, braces the powers into unity, and gives stability to all the virtues. As the tree obtains its strength from being rooted in the ground, the soul, which is the tree of virtue, obtains its strength from patiently adhering to God.

Patience is concerned in all that we have to resist, in all that we have to deny ourselves, in all that we have to endure, in all that we have to adhere to, and in all that we have to do. Wherever patience fails, the act is weak, and the work imperfect.

Recognize sufferings as opportunities for patience

The first thing to understand is that patience is an immediate exercise of the will, which is the spring of all free and moral actions. It must not, therefore, be confounded with the sentiments, sensibilities, or feelings, because it is a pure act of the will. When the will rests on God, looks to God, and draws strength from God, the patience which resists all evils and disorders, gives us the possession of ourselves, and keeps the soul in peace is generated. "Be thou, O my soul, subject to God, for from Him is my patience."[26]

The first movements of impatience, the first uneasiness of dissatisfaction, are warnings to patience to be on its guard, lest trouble arise to disturb the soul and take

[26]Ps. 61:6 (RSV = Ps. 62:5).

hold of the will. If we calmly look down from the superior soul upon the first movements of irritation or impatience, nothing can appear more contemptible; and under the rebuke of the gaze of our interior eye they vanish in shame. The breath of patience will disperse the little cloud of trouble and discontent that moves in our lower nature, but if left to itself, it will quickly grow on what it feeds upon, and will envelop and fill the soul with anger and vexation. For anger is a brooding vice that feeds on sensitive self-love and imaginary wrong far beyond the original offense — if, indeed, offense has been given.

∞

There is nothing that drives us to impatience so vehemently, or throws us into greater interior disorder, than an injury, or the imagination of an injury, which is far more frequent than real injury. For many things are said and done without the least intention of injury — some from quickness of tongue, some from inadvertence or thoughtlessness, some in good-natured jest, some from good intentions, and some from mere imprudence — and no one has any right to take offense at any of them, and so commit himself to anger, grief, and sadness. But if anyone should falsely or maliciously assail our good name and reputation — a mode of detraction not limited to the children of this world — let us, in that case, keep our magnanimity, so that our virtue may be stronger than another's vice, and that our patience may suffer no loss by reason of another's improbity. Rather, we should rejoice in the Lord, that He has called us by these means to greater justice, which is commonly born, receives its growth, and obtains perfection among injuries and insults.

When things are at their worst according to the world, if the calamity is rightly used, things begin to be at their best according to God. All things are in God's hands, to give or take as He chooses; and an immortal soul is more precious in His sight than all that the world can give. When He strips a soul of earthly things, He calls upon that soul to look to Him and to trust in His care and Providence.

There is nothing really lost so long as God is with us; nothing, therefore, of which to despair. As long as we are simple, upright, fearing God and departing from evil, placing our hope in God and not in the prudence of the world, He who has care of His servants will turn our calamities into blessings.

The only good we have that is excellent and imperishable is our soul, and the good that God gives to the soul. But by nothing except our own will can the soul or its good suffer injury. No one can be spiritually injured except by himself. So long as we possess our soul in patience,[27] no one can take any part of that good away from us. We can only lose the good of the soul by not holding to it with constancy, and we thus sin by losing patience.

Sadness is the most selfish of all selfish things, and the very essence of self — consuming the very heart of virtue. When sadness is much indulged in, there follows a contraction of mind, a weakening of the soul's power, a dissolving of the heart's strength, and an embittering of the spirit, which causes restless discomfort, and brings forth indignation and melancholy.

God knows what we need far better than we know ourselves. Our trials are the fatherly dispositions of His

[27]Cf. Luke 21:19.

Recognize sufferings as opportunities

Providence, and it is idle to fix our mind on human causes, when those causes are ruled by God as He seeks to bring about changes in us. They are brought upon us for our probation, our correction, or the expiation of our sins. They purge those noxious temperaments, the products of self-love and sloth, which obstruct and impede the generous flow of spiritual life. They plant in us the seed of merit, and prepare the rewards of endurance. They make us generous in conforming our will to the will of God. Hence the cheerful endurance of trials and sufferings is a virtue truly sublime, reaching its heroic degrees in the martyrs and confessors of God.

We are made to enjoy God. But we must be purified before we can be sanctified; and we must deserve God, as far as we are able, by becoming more like His Incarnate Son, crucified in spirit as well as in body.

Be it understood and remembered that the darkness of trial is not evil, that dryness of spirit is not sin, and that confusion of mind is not malice. They are invitations to patience, calls to resignation, beckonings to the healing Cross, and admonitions to be humble and

Patience and Humility

obedient to the will of God. But if in our interior trials we lose patience, then we fall into sadness, and so become weak, troubled, and discouraged. The remedy for sadness is prayer. God is secretly present with the suffering soul, and in reward for patience, it receives a secret strength and peace.

Strive to quiet your soul

One color cannot make a picture, nor one virtue a saint; many colors unite and blend their shades to form a beautiful work of art, and many virtues unite and blend together in happy mixture to make a beautiful soul.

All the Christian virtues live in the light of faith, all look to hope, and all obtain their life from the love of God. They are founded in humility, sustained by fortitude, strengthened and protected by patience.

A soul given to impatience loses strength from every virtue and weakens its hold on all that is good; it has not the spiritual nerve to hold itself together; for in the impatient soul there is a restlessness, a wavering, a want of spiritual fiber, a swerving from good intention, and a want of steadfastness in action that disturbs the soul.

Patience and Humility

∞

All the present conditions of life seem to combine in making men restless and unstable. Most men have become eager for novelty and change, and they live so much outside themselves as to neglect or even abandon the interior good of their souls. The tree of knowledge of good and evil[28] has been shaken for its fruits, and if the knowledge of God has fallen to those who are inclined to God, the knowledge of evil has fallen in great abundance to those who are inclined to evil. We live in the midst of a restless, impatient, and fevered life, which more than ever demands for our security patience of will and stability of mind.

∞

Food is not more essential to strength of body than patience is to strength of soul; and God in His goodness makes us conscious of our weakness, so that we may be induced to seek the means of strength. What God loves and approves in us is the cheerful and loving

[28]Gen. 2:9.

patience that we put into our duties, because that is the spirit of charity, and it expresses the amount of charity with which we serve Him. Every new restraint that we put upon the hurry and impetuosity of our excitable nature is a reduction to order, a power gained, a weakness removed, a further subjection of that nature to grace, and a step in the way of peace, which makes us less unlike God. The secret of cheerfulness and content is in the freedom of spirit obtained by the conquest of the body.

There is also an impatience with oneself; and who is not acquainted with that infirmity? It may have its beginning in some venial fault or error into which we have slipped or glided with no great deliberation. But the failure has wounded our self-love, and produced an interior annoyance and vexation, which is far worse than the original fault. Like throwing away the medicine when the disease appears, we give up patience at the very moment when it is wanted to cure our infirmity. Had we taken to that steadying virtue at once, the mischief would have been stayed; but the shame

Patience and Humility

and humiliation of failure is allowed to disturb the heart, to discomfort the soul, and to bring on a certain sadness that goes from one act of interior impatience to another, doing more harm than a hundred of those faults from which this disorder is allowed to rise. Patience would have purged the sin, and would have saved us from it in future. We must therefore take hold of patience, or the one fault will bring us greater ones in its train.

Let nothing disturb your soul

The greatest moral strength of which the soul is capable comes of the Christian grace and gift of fortitude, of which patience is a potential part; that is to say, it agrees with patience in some respects and differs from it in others.

Patience is mostly concerned in overcoming the restlessness of nature, in enduring adversities, in resisting temptations, and in subduing or keeping away impatience, anger, and sadness. Fortitude is a braver and a stronger virtue, is more deeply woven into the constitutions of the soul, and is concerned with difficult action as well as with difficult endurance. Fortitude is required to face great dangers bravely, to undertake great works beset with difficulties, or to undergo martyrdom or the equivalent of martyrdom. Fortitude is a virtue more deeply seated in the soul, more calm in its operations, and less the subject of consciousness than patience.

∞

The world admires its own heroes, who, for honor, interest or the excitement which it gives them, undergo great labors, do works that look large in the eyes of men, encounter great perils with risk of life, or endure extreme sufferings for some public cause. And although these men are not infrequently known to have their moral deficiencies and failings, yet the world exalts them, rewards them with honors and benefits, and erects monuments to their memory. The hope of these things is often the leading motive, next to the pride that moves within them.

But the heroes and heroines of God, although the world takes little note of them, are far more wonderful. Armed with Christian fortitude, their hearts are set on God, in whose strength they do great things,[29] and, while wholly indifferent to the world's opinion, are a spectacle to God and His angels.

[29]Cf. Phil. 4:13.

Let nothing disturb your soul

In their valiant combats they first conquer themselves, that they may be in a position to surmount all outward dangers and difficulties. They have no fears but the fear of God, and no will but His will. Let but the will of God be known, and, however difficult the task may be to human nature, no fear, no obstacle will daunt their ardor in accomplishing His will. The way of God in His servants is the way of fortitude in humility.

∞

Of all the burdens laid upon us in this life, the heaviest is our own body, and this is owing to the just law which God passed upon that old sin, which is so widely known but so little understood. The soul trembles and quakes with fear, lest our body be vexed or tormented with pain or labor, or be taken from us by death.

Through the mere custom of always carrying the body, we love the burden of it, and find it hard to realize that, if through the help of the law of divine love, we govern the body wisely and well, it will obtain its resurrection and salvation, and its rights will suffer no injury. But when the soul is turned to God with the fortitude of love, these things become known and death is not only endured, but welcomed with desire. There remains the great conflict with pain and suffering, yet nothing of this kind is of such iron hardness and obstinacy that the fire of love cannot master it. When this fire bears the soul toward God, the soul soars up freely and wonderfully on strong and beautiful wings over every torment inflicted on the body, until its chaste desire brings it to rest in the embrace of God.

∞

Can we ever allow that God would permit the lovers of money, or of praise, or of sensual pleasure, to become stronger than His own lovers? Their affections are not love — they deserve no other name than that of concupiscence or lust — yet they show what a force the soul can put forth, even in the heated and noxious pursuit of those poor objects.

But this is an argument for us, for if the lovers of these things can endure so much while deserting God for the sake of them, how much more ought we to be ready to endure to save us from the unhappiness of deserting God.

Let nothing disturb your soul

A life of self-denial is a martyrdom. The life of the true Christian is a daily cross and martyrdom. To deny ourselves, to combat the corrupt propensities of our nature, to keep the desire of eternity well advanced before the things of time, and to endure whatever may come upon us, demands a patience, a fortitude, and a perseverance like the force that carried the martyrs through their sufferings.

Softness comes of ease and pleasure. A soft and easy life melts away those energies whereby we endure labors and hardships, and dissolves the force that encounters, and conquers the difficulties that we meet in doing good works, and especially in doing them in the best and most perfect way. The proper cure for the contemptible vice of softness is labor and self-denial.

Whatever befalls you, let it not upset or disturb your mind. The whole world cannot injure a soul that is fenced with faithful fortitude.

Draw near to the suffering Christ

Of all that God has taught us, and of all we have learned by experience, there is nothing that strikes the reflecting mind with more awe and wonder, or proves more fully His perfection, than God's infinite patience with His rebellious and sinful creatures. To the eyes of faith, this very patience is one of the sublimest proofs of the divine perfections. As the Lord of men, Jesus Christ became their teacher, and He exhorts us to take up our daily cross, and to follow Him with patience.[30]

Severe to Himself, He is gentle, mild, and forbearing to all others. His meekness is the beautiful flower, His peacefulness the sweet fruit of His patience. His doctrine is doubted and disputed; He is charged with being an impostor; He is called a blasphemer; His

[30]Matt. 16:24; Luke 9:23.

wonderful works are ascribed to the Devil; His adversaries gnash their teeth, burn with rage and are prepared to stone Him. Yet His equanimity is unmoved, His meek demeanor is not altered, and the calmness of His peace undergoes no change. Resting on His union with His Father, the ground of His invincible strength, His divine fortitude is tried at every point, and at every point His patience is invincible.

∞

If we enter into the interior of the Son of God, we shall there find a crucifixion of the soul sustained by a charity most patient because most divine. Nothing can be so helpful to souls under interior trials as to enter in spirit into the interior crucifixion of our Blessed Lord. He thirsts for the salvation of all whom, by His Incarnation, He has made His brethren; and the resistance that He meets with from the pride of self-seeking wills causes Him the greatest anguish of spirit.

Whenever we draw near to the suffering Son of God, and put our heart into that furnace of love and patience, we receive a light, an affection, and an unction that soothes all sorrows into peace, cleanses the soul from evil, and comforts it with a cordial strength and an ever-increasing desire of the eternal good. The world is full of mysteries; the soul is full of mysteries; Heaven is all mystery to us earthly creatures. But whoever embraces the cross with open heart finds therein the explanation of a thousand mysteries.

∞

We profess to be the patient followers of the patient Son of God. Do we understand how deep that patience goes which rests the humanity of Christ upon the firm foundation of His divinity, and gives to His human will the strength to hold to the will of His Father, unmoved and undisturbed in its peace and self-possession by all that men can say or do against Him? Do we understand the profundity of that patience which refrains from every egotistical self-assertion, however grossly He is misjudged, however ignominiously He is insulted? He only glorifies His heavenly Father, declares His unity with His Father, and equally declares that He can do nothing without His Father. Yet He calls upon us to be the imitators of His patience, to rest for strength on Him; to take up our daily cross and follow Him; to refrain

Patience and Humility

from our selfish egotism; and in patience to possess our souls.

As the patient sufferings of our Lord were the cause of His glory, similar patience in sufferings will bring us to His glory.

School yourself in patience

What is it to hold our soul in our own possession? As we have not our resources from ourselves, because we are not created for ourselves, but for God, we cannot possess our soul except in God. We possess our mind in the light of His truth, and our will in the grace of His love. Hence when Adam fell from God, he lost the possession of himself. So long as our mind adheres to God in His truth, and our will adheres to God in His love, we are in possession of ourselves. But if we follow the seductions of error, we lose the possession of ourselves. As our mortal life is only free and self-possessed when we live in light and air, our spiritual life is only free and self-possessed when we live in the truth and love of God.

Patience is the possession of the soul, enabling the will to keep the soul in peace, and to regulate its actions and desires by the light of truth and justice, with a constant view to its final end. Impatience is the beginning of every movement that takes the soul away from God, and so from its self-possession.

∞

The greatest thing for us is the perfection of our own soul; and the saints teach us that this perfection consists in doing our ordinary actions well. We do them well when we do them patiently and lovingly. We have to perfect our ordinary actions for the love of God, that we may be perfect in our human way before our heavenly Father, as He is most perfect in His divine way. But it is the patience of charity that makes our actions perfect. It is not the habit or exercise of patience alone that gives perfection to our actions, but rather it is patience proceeding from charity, and working in the spirit and abundance of charity.

∞

The first rule for acquiring patience is to hold its value in great estimation, and to have a great desire of it.

School yourself in patience

The second rule is to begin the exercise of patience with our own interior, and to direct our chief attention to the controlling of our interior powers. For this virtue must be strong at home before it can be strong abroad.

The third rule is the government of the tongue, which is the surest test of the custody of the heart. Let thought go before speech, not speech before thought. The tree is known by its fruits, and man by his speech. Much talkativeness is the sign of a feeble mind, and an undisciplined will. The tongue is the great disturber of our peace, and of the peace of other souls.

The fourth rule of patience is to keep all things in their just and due order. To be careless about the order of external things is the sign of an ill-regulated mind, St. Bonaventure[31] says.

The fifth rule is to bear patiently with those whose tempers are infirm, and to endure their tempers with charitable kindness.

The sixth rule is to manage wisely our own infirmities of temper. The provocation may arise within ourselves, or it may come from the voice or conduct of

[31]St. Bonaventure (c. 1217-1274), Franciscan theologian and Doctor of the Church.

another. Whichever it may be, the true cause of evil temper is always in oneself. One who is habitually recollected in God cannot easily be moved to anger. Resting his soul on its divine foundation, he enjoys a peace which makes his soul quickly sensible of the first movements of disturbance and quick to turn from them, so that they cannot overwhelm his soul.

The seventh rule is given by St. Paul: "Be not overcome by evil, but overcome evil by good."[32]

The eighth rule of patience is to bear our interior trials, crosses, and aridities with peace and resignation.

The ninth rule of patience, and one of very great importance, is to bear patiently with one's own faults and failures. Unless we bear our failings with patience, they will lead us into numberless faults.

The tenth and last rule is that of the perfect, who find a cheering joy in trials, contradictions, and sufferings, not only because they are great helps for advancing toward God upon the groundworks of humility and patience, but also because they can find nothing more conducive to detachment from all that is not God; nothing more effective in subduing their nature to the reign

[32]Rom. 12:21.

of grace. They delight in bearing upon them the marks of Christ crucified.[33] This is a degree of fortitude more than human, a singular gift of the Holy Spirit, by which the superior will is so closely united with God as to remove all repugnance to suffering.

[33]Cf. Gal. 6:17.

Work with cheerful patience

That perfection of life consists in doing our ordinary actions well is one of the wisest maxims of the saints. Those duties make up the chief sum of our lives during the time allotted to us in this world. As we owe our life and time to God, the good Christian has duties at all hours.

The perfection of our ordinary actions depends on high motives, good will, and cheerful patience. High motives give our ordinary actions their value before God; good will makes them vigorous; cheerful patience makes them orderly, peaceful, effective, and pleasant. Hence the poor man who goes to his daily toils with good will and cheerful patience for the love of God is a much nobler person in the sight of God than the man who, from mere human motives, shines with splendid actions in the sight of the world.

Patience and Humility

∞

Whatever we do is perfect in proportion to the self-possession with which we do it, and that self-possession is proportioned to patience. Nothing, however trifling, can be done well without good judgment. There are fifty ways of doing anything, but only one perfect way. Nature is always inclined to hurry, to run before judgment, but grace is deliberate. To work fruitfully is to work with a patient will; fretful haste damages both the work and the workman.

Those who are patient with obstacles will be patient when the work runs smoothly.

There are few greater proofs of a well-disciplined interior than to be able to break off at any time with cheerfulness from one duty and to turn with equal cheerfulness to another, however unexpected the interruption may be. It is an effect of that detachment of will that comes of patient charity.

∞

In order that our offices of kindness and charity may have all their sweetness, beauty, and consolation, they must proceed with direct simplicity from the love of God in the heart. The love of God is the most earnest and most practical of all things; and when it is devoted with sincerity to the service of our neighbors, it places us in a sublime position that has more of Heaven than of earth in it. We enter into God's charity when we imitate His patient love toward all who come within our sphere of action.

Beware of anxiety. Next to sin, there is nothing that so much troubles the mind, strains the heart, distresses the soul, and confuses the judgment. Anxiety is not in the things about which we are anxious. It is caused by taking our solicitudes and uncertainties into our own interior and there making them the subject of our troubled, disquieted, and overstrained feelings.

There is but one remedy for anxiety, and that is by using the firm force of patience to keep the objects of our solicitude in their proper place; and that place is outside the feelings and before the mind. Every advancement in humility and patience removes the causes of anxiety and trouble, because they all have their roots in the restless impatience of sensitive self-love.

In all your affairs and responsibilities, rest wholly on the Providence of God, who alone can bring your

Patience and Humility

plans to a happy conclusion. Yet do your best in a peaceful way to follow the guidance of God's Providence, and then be assured that if your trust has been in God, whatever success you may obtain will be all the more profitable to you, whatever you yourself may be inclined to think of it.

Whenever you are perplexed as to what course you should take, if you go blindly into action, you will be sure to repent of it. Wait for light, wait with patience, and light will not fail you.

Endure suffering patiently

There are two Christian virtues whose names sound unpleasant to the sensual man. Humility is one of them, and patience is the other. Self-love and impatience are cowardly vices that shrink with insane fear from the health-giving labors of humility and patience.

So completely does the habit of patience form and perfect the character of the Christian man, so thoroughly does it furnish the test of his faith as well as of his charity, that St. Paul has not failed to point this out in his own example to his favorite disciple, Timothy.[34]

What is perfect is unchangeable. The patience of God is unchangeable. But we, with our little patience, are the subjects of time and change, and impatience always changes us for the worst. Change, like death, destroys

[34]Cf. 2 Tim 4:6-7.

what went before. If the change comes from God, it is a happy change; it makes us better than before. If it comes from impatience, it makes us worse than before. But by union with the unchangeable God, whereby we always change to better things, whoever adheres to God is saved by patience from the changes that make us worse.

"In your patience you shall possess your soul."[35] Every man is a man only insofar as he holds the free possession of his soul. Every woman is truly a woman only insofar as she possesses her soul in peace. The Christian is a true Christian only insofar as he possesses his soul in God, so that the world cannot take hold of him. And the secret of this self-possession is in the patience which gives him a beautiful resemblance to Christ.

The words, "Thy will be done,"[36] when they spring from the surrender of all to God, bring to the soul a peace and courage that are not without a taste of the goodness

[35]Luke 21:19.
[36]Matt. 6:10.

of God. Why are great trials allowed, except to bring the soul to devout acts of resignation? This pure resignation brings the soul straight to God, establishes it in God, and makes it conformable to God. True devotion, therefore, consists in true and most humble resignation. Those who strive most vigorously against themselves, although they may leave this world imperfect and have to be purified in the next, will obtain a much higher place in Heaven than those who have not striven with the same energy and patience, even though these last should reach Heaven without any need of purgation.

∞

There is nothing that we suffer for the honor of God, however little it may be, that is not more serviceable to us than if we possessed the dominion of the world. But suffering must be unselfish. God would not have us suffer anything for His sake that is not both useful and fruitful to ourselves. However great our trial or affliction may be, the Son of God bore them first, and permits them for our good.

Christ not only perfected His own patience by His sufferings, but He receives all the sufferings endured by

Patience and Humility

His members for His sake, incorporates them with His own, endows them with His merits, and thus gives them a communion with His own proportioned to their loving patience. For in virtue of His grace and love they are made sacred and holy.

Pray from your heart

The path of prayer is the king's highway from earth to Heaven. While the body remains on its kindred earth, the spirit ascends on the wings of grace into that divine region of light and good for which it was created. This royal path leads the soul into the eternal presence, there to plead its cause with its Creator and sovereign Lord; to converse in the humble spirit of childlike affection with its heavenly Father; and to receive His good and perfect gifts.

This royal highway to God was opened for us by our Lord Jesus Christ, was consecrated by His prayers and sufferings, and was illuminated by His Ascension into Heaven through the path which He opened. By His Incarnation He bridged the whole distance between the creature and the Creator. He is Himself the way, the light of the way, and its security. Through Him we have access to the Father, who answers us with mercy and benignity. "I go to the Father: and whatsoever you ask the Father in my name I will do, that the Father may be glorified in the Son."[37]

∞

Prayer is, therefore, the noblest and most exalted action of which man is capable through the grace of God. It is the action of God's created image seeking union with its divine original, and seeking it so that this image may be healed from offense, be perfected into likeness by the reception of life from the eternal life, and be prepared for beatitude through the gifts that descend from God's infinite perfection. The voices that reach the ears of God are not words but desires. If we seek the eternal life with our lips, without desiring that life with our heart, our outcry is nothing but silence. But when we desire that life from our heart, although our mouth be silent, in that silence we cry to God.

The great obstacles to prayer are self-love, the inconstancy of the will, and the sadness that results from

[37]John 14:13.

self-love and inconstancy. Self-love draws our senses, thought, and will to ourselves, instead of surrendering them to God and to the guidance of His Holy Spirit. This causes the will to swing like a pendulum — but in a very unsteady way — between God and oneself, making the soul restless, impatient, inattentive, and wandering. Yet we cannot look to God and to ourselves at the same time; we cannot seek God and ourselves at the same moment. This is not pure prayer, but prayer mixed with distractions, self-love, and confusion.

The Holy Spirit is the true teacher of prayer, and the liberty of prayer consists in freely following the divine attraction, which always leads to greater simplicity, humility, love, patience, and union with God. "Commit thy way to the Lord, and trust in Him. . . . Be subject to the Lord and pray to Him."[38]

All prayer has one final end — beatitude in God — and should be exercised in spirit and in truth. Every kind of prayer leads to interior recollection according to

[38]Ps. 36:5, 7 (RSV = Ps. 37: 5, 7).

each one's gift and disposition, and when this recollection ascends to contemplation, the summit of prayer is reached. Contemplation rises above the senses, above the imagination, and above all processes of the reasoning powers. Collected within itself, the soul rises above itself, and with a simple view beholds, although "darkly as through a glass,"[39] some manifestation of the beauty, goodness, and greatness of God, which deepens its sense of God. The acts of contemplation are four: to seek after God, to find Him, to feel His sacred touch in the soul, and to be united with Him and enjoy Him.

[39]Cf. 1 Cor. 13:12.

Be patient in prayer

As that which is weak is strengthened by resting on what is strong, the soul is made strong by resting with its interior center upon the strengthening power of God. "Be thou, O my soul, subject to God: for from Him is my patience."[40] What is restless by nature can be made calm and peaceful only by union with what is calm and peaceful. We obtain peace from our troubles by union with the God of peace. "It is good for me to adhere to God, to set my hope on the Lord God."[41]

As we can obtain stability of mind and heart only by union with what is unchangeable, our soul obtains stability by union with the unchangeable God. The principle of that union is charity, and God has placed the

[40]Ps. 61:6 (RSV = Ps. 62:5).
[41]Ps. 72:28 (Ps. 73:28).

power of patience in the gift of charity, that we may be able to adhere with our spirit to Him in a firm, stable, and patient love. "Charity is patient."[42]

∞

Whatever is created is made for an object and an end which is different from itself, and from which it receives its fullness, peace, and perfection. God has created us for Himself, and only by union with God can we receive our fullness, peace, and perfection. This union we seek in prayer, and by prayer we prepare ourselves for our eternal union with God.

It is of great importance to understand what we ought to put into our prayer, for the value and merit of our good works depend less on their show than on the spirit and virtue put into them.

The first condition of prayer is attention, which signifies a stretching forth. We stretch forth the ear to listen, the eye to see, and the mind to understand.

The second condition is humility, whereby the soul is opened and made subject to God.

[42] 1 Cor. 13:4.

The third condition is faith in God, and trust that He will hear our prayer, and grant it according to His promises.

The fourth condition is the love of God, which makes our prayer generous and acceptable.

The fifth condition is obedience to the interior movements of the Holy Spirit.

The sixth condition is patience. This virtue should be present throughout every good prayer.

Let anyone who would feel the value of patient prayer take the Our Father or the Creed, or a Hymn to the Holy Spirit and repeat it slowly and attentively, with the heart on God and the mind on the sense of the prayer. He will find, perhaps with some surprise, how much more light will come to his mind, how much more sweetness will come to his heart, and how much nearer to God he will feel, than when these customary prayers are little better than gabbled without their full and solemn sense.

Be cheerful

There can be no better proof of a healthy soul than habitual cheerfulness. Christian cheerfulness is that modest, hopeful, and peaceful joy which springs from charity and is protected by patience. It is the well-regulated vigor of spiritual life that throws off all morbid moods and depressing influences, refusing them a lodging in the soul devoted to God. Cheerfulness gives freedom to our thoughts and a generous spirit to our actions. It makes our services to God acceptable, and our services to our neighbor grateful. "God loveth the cheerful giver."[43]

This cheerfulness of soul springs from the divine good which God has placed in us, which acts in us, and of which we are partakers. Hence purity of conscience

[43] 2 Cor. 9:7.

is a great promoter of cheerfulness, for when the conscience is clean, the affections are pure. But the moving cause of cheerfulness is in the exercise of the virtues, especially because they are the ready servants of the joy of loving God. Yet even the joy of charity is very imperfect, and is often troubled, unless that charity is patient.

If we had no greater joys than the world can give the body, or the body can give the soul, we would be poor creatures indeed — nothing but animals. If we had no greater enjoyment than the material scientists can give us, we would be unhappy creatures. Poring over matter until they lose sight of their immortal souls, they materialize their souls, and wish to materialize us. Losing the power of ascending from the creature to the Creator, by an immense abuse of their intelligence they drown their souls in their senses, cast a shadow of gloom and sadness over the world, and do their best to make it a dreary habitation for immortal souls.

The Christian soul lives in communion with God, and to that soul a prospect is opened into infinite and unchangeable truth. Within that soul a sense is opened that tastes the infinite and eternal God. What opens this eye to the soul? The light of faith descending from God. What awakes this sense in the soul? The grace of charity from the Holy Spirit of God. Can anything be so cheering to the soul as its growth in truth except its growth in good?

As truth and good come to our soul from God, can anything secure their increase like prayer and communion with God? By this holy association, hope of greater things to come is always growing. Unlike our association with the world, it is inexhaustible in expectation of eternal God.

The children of the world, who live for themselves, know nothing of the enjoyments of the children of grace, who live for God. Bent upon the things beneath them, their enjoyment comes from nothing that is equal to their spiritual nature; and what they do enjoy contains the seeds of sadness and decay.

Loving only mortal things with an immortal soul, they pervert the order of their nature until their desires contradict their wants. The flowers of their gladness fade and die, and the fruits of sadness come in their place.

Patience and Humility

∞

Nothing contributes more to cheerfulness than the habit of looking at the good side of things. The good side is God's side of them. But even on their human side, what makes them appear worse than they are is conferred on them by the envy, jealousy, and malice of our hearts, falsely imagining that what depresses others exalts ourselves. Let patience keep down envy and repress the fancy of our own superiority.

Cheerfulness implies hope, courage, confidence in God, the turning a deaf ear to the complaints of self-love, and a certain modest joy in the consciousness that in the hands of God, "in whom we live, and move, and have our being,"[44] we are safe.

Why should we not rejoice in the good things of God? We can rejoice in the good things of the senses; why not in the good things of the soul? If the day is pure and serene, we enjoy its gladness. Why should we not rejoice in the serene light of truth that shines from Heaven upon our minds? Why should we not delight in the beautiful gifts of God? Having an almighty and

[44]Acts 17:28.

most loving Father, let us rejoice in Him. Having a most loving Savior, truly God, who has made Himself our brother, and feeds us with His life, we ought surely to rejoice in Him. Having the Holy Spirit of God with us, dwelling in us with wonderful condescension, making us His temples, and pouring His love into our hearts, we ought certainly to answer His love and rejoice in His overflowing goodness. Why should we ever set a gloomy face against a guest so beautiful and generous?

The great enemy of the soul is not trial but sadness, which is the bleeding wound of self-love.

"We may always rejoice," observes St. Chrysostom, "if we will only keep our head a little raised above the flood of human things."[45]

---

[45]St. John Chrysostom (c. 347-407), Bishop of Constantinople and Doctor of the Church.

William Bernard Ullathorne, O.S.B. (1806-1889)

William Bernard Ullathorne, born in Yorkshire, England, in 1806, was a descendant of St. Thomas More and of other Catholics who stayed true to their Faith during a time when many were falling away owing to Protestant persecution. This heritage was to reveal itself later in life, when Ullathorne worked unceasingly for the restoration of the Catholic hierarchy in England.

Becoming enamored of the sea at a young age, Ullathorne worked as a cabin boy for most of his youth, but he was eventually led in 1823 to enter the Benedictine order at Downside, where he was ordained a priest seven years later. From that time on, he led the life of an active and zealous missionary, both in Australia and, later, closer to home in Coventry, until he was named Vicar Apostolic of the western half of England

Patience and Humility

in 1846, Bishop of Birmingham in 1850, and, finally, Titular Archbishop of Cabasa.

Although he is known for his aggressive apostolic zeal, Archbishop Ullathorne is perhaps best remembered for his famous — and all-encompassing — spiritual treatise *The Groundwork of the Christian Virtues*. He writes in an engaging and practical yet earnest manner that conveys to the reader the importance of the virtues — particularly humility — and the daily struggles and opportunities that are involved in achieving holiness.

Your generosity can help Sophia Institute Press® to provide the public with editions of works containing the enduring wisdom of the ages. Please send your tax-deductible contribution to the address below.

The members of the Editorial Board of Sophia Institute Press® welcome questions, comments, and suggestions from all our readers.

For your free catalog, call:
Toll-free: 1-800-888-9344

or write:
Sophia Institute Press®
Box 5284
Manchester, NH 03108

or visit our website at:
http://www.sophiainstitute.com

Sophia Institute Press®

Sophia Institute is a nonprofit institution that seeks to restore man's knowledge of eternal truth, including man's knowledge of his own nature, his relation to other persons, and his relation to God.

Sophia Institute Press® serves this end in numerous ways. It publishes translations of foreign works to make them accessible for the first time to English-speaking readers. It brings back into print books that have been long out of print. And it publishes important new books that fulfill the ideals of Sophia Institute. These books afford readers a rich source of the enduring wisdom of mankind.

Sophia Institute Press® makes these high-quality books available to the general public by using advanced technology and by soliciting donations to subsidize its general publishing costs.